AFRICAN ANIMALS

A TRUE BOOK

by

Ann O. Squire

Children's Press®
A Division of Scholastic Inc.

New York Toronto London Auckland Sydney
Mexico City New Delhi Hong Kong
Danbury, Connecticut

A lioness and her cubs

Content Consultant
Kathy Carlstead, Ph.D.
Honolulu Zoo

Reading Consultant
Nanci R. Vargus, Ed.D.
Primary Multiage Teacher
Decatur Township Schools,
Indianapolis, IN

Dedication
To Evan

The photograph on the cover
shows African elephants.
The photograph on the title
page shows two mandrills.

Library of Congress Cataloging-in-Publication Data

Squire, Ann.
    African animals / by Ann O. Squire.
        p. cm. — (A True book)
    Includes bibliographical references (p.).
    ISBN 0-516-22187-6 (lib. bdg.)   0-516-25994-6 (pbk.)
    1. Zoology—Africa—Juvenile literature. [1. Zoology—Africa.] I. Title.
II. Series.

QL336.S68 2001
591.96—dc21   00-57028

GROLIER
PUBLISHING

1 2 3 4 5 6 7 8 9 10 R 10 09 08 07 06 05 04 03 02 01

Contents

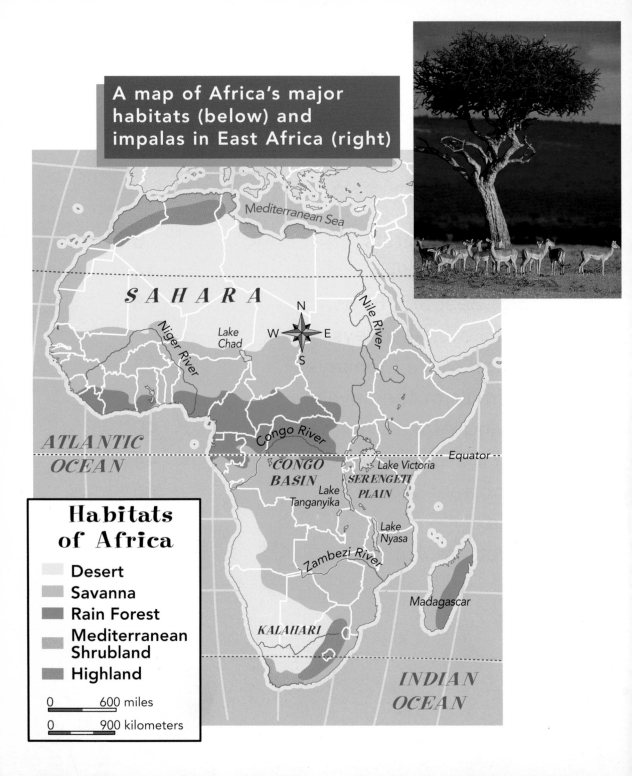

A map of Africa's major habitats (below) and impalas in East Africa (right)

Mediterranean Sea

SAHARA

Niger River

Lake Chad

Nile River

N
W   E
S

ATLANTIC OCEAN

Congo River

Equator

CONGO BASIN

Lake Victoria

SERENGETI PLAIN

Lake Tanganyika

Lake Nyasa

Zambezi River

Madagascar

KALAHARI

INDIAN OCEAN

Habitats of Africa

- Desert
- Savanna
- Rain Forest
- Mediterranean Shrubland
- Highland

0   600 miles

0   900 kilometers

African Habitats

What do you think Africa is like? Is it a hot, dry desert? Or is it a dark, damp jungle? Deserts and jungles are just two of the habitats found on this huge continent. Africa is made up of many different countries, and many different habitats as well.

One African habitat, for example, is the savanna—a dry grassy plain. Grazing animals such as gazelles, zebras, and giraffes live on Africa's savannas. Meat-eating animals, like lions and chee-tahs, live there too. East Africa's Serengeti Plain is one of the world's best-known savannas.

A very dry savanna is called a desert. Northern Africa contains large areas of desert,

Animals of the African savanna include gazelles (above), giraffes (left), and zebras (below).

The Sahara Desert

including the Sahara, the largest hot desert on Earth. The fennec fox, the striped hyena, and the desert monitor are among the many animals that live in the Sahara Desert.

The monitor (above) and the fennec fox (left) are among the animals of Africa's Sahara Desert.

Gorillas (above) live in the rain forests of central Africa. Many brightly colored birds, including the purple-crested turaco (left), can be found in Africa's forests.

Africa's forests are full of low shrubs, vines, and towering trees. Forests that get a lot of rain are called tropical rain forests. Gorillas, chimpanzees, and many other primates live in the forests.

African forests are also home to many brightly colored birds, giant bugs, fruit-eating bats, and other amazing creatures. Dense forests can be found in many areas of Central and West Africa.

Wetlands are lakes, rivers, and swamps. In Africa's wetlands live hippos, crocodiles,

Wetland animals include hippos and many kinds of birds (top). Thirsty savanna animals come to the wetlands to drink (bottom).

fish, and huge flocks of pink flamingos. Many savanna animals come to these wetlands to drink.

12

Long Live the Tortoises

A tortoise is a turtle that lives on land. Radiated tortoises come from the island of Madagascar, off the east coast of Africa. They are among the longest-lived animals in the world. The oldest radiated tortoise on record died in 1966 at the ripe old age of 189.

Hidden Wildlife

Some of Africa's most interesting animals are also the most difficult to spot. A small but deadly killer called the assassin bug prowls the forest looking for bees, flies, and other victims.

Once this bug has made a catch, it pierces its prey's body with its long mouthparts. Then it

An assassin bug
attacking a beetle

injects a substance that turns
its prey's insides into a liquidy
"soup." Finally, the assassin
bug drinks the "soup," using
its mouthparts as a straw.

The Goliath beetle is a giant among African insects. Weighing in at over 3 ounces (85 grams)—about the size of a small apple—it is one of the heaviest insects in the world. Amazingly, the Goliath beetle can fly!

Many kinds of fish are found in the rivers of Africa, but few are as unusual as the upside-down catfish. Most catfish stay close to the river bottom, searching for food with their long, whiskerlike feelers. The

upside-down catfish does just the opposite. This weird fish swims along on its back, just beneath the water's surface, to find its food.

Big, Beautiful Birds

The largest bird in the world lives on the African savanna. An ostrich can be nearly 9 feet (2.7 meters) tall and weigh up to 350 pounds (159 kilograms). Because of its large size—not to mention its small wings— the ostrich cannot fly. But its long, strong legs make this

Male (top left) and female (top right) ostriches;
Ostriches can run as fast as 45 mi. (72 km) per hour.

bird a champion runner. An ostrich can zip across the plains at a speed of 45 miles (72 kilometers) per hour.

A flock of flamingos in Kenya

Ostriches live in small groups. Flamingos, however, live in huge flocks of as many as one million birds.

Flamingos are always found near water, such as shallow lakes or marshes. Standing on their long, thin legs, they stretch their necks down to the water to feed on fish, insects, crustaceans, and plants. In the wild, these birds get their pink color from the food they eat— shrimp and algae. In zoos,

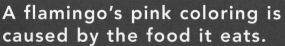
A flamingo's pink coloring is caused by the food it eats.

flamingos are given special foods to keep them "in the pink." Without these foods, the birds would soon fade to white.

The red-billed hornbill is one of Africa's most unusual birds. At mating time, the female hornbill finds a hole in a tree, climbs inside, and lays her eggs. Then she does something really odd. She seals up the entrance to her nest with mud, leaving only a tiny slit. While she sits on her eggs, the male passes food to her through the opening. During the weeks it takes for the eggs to hatch,

A male red-billed hornbill passing bark to a female sealed inside her nest

the mother hornbill is a prisoner inside her own nest. But her eggs are safe!

24

Monkeys, Monkeys, and More Monkeys

Monkeys and apes live all over Africa, from the dry desert of Ethiopia to the misty rain forests of Congo. The world's most colorful mammal, the mandrill, lives in these dense forests.

25

A male mandrill

Once you've seen a male mandrill, you'll never forget the sight. It has a bright-red nose with patches of sky blue on each side. The mandrill's rear end is the same bright blue color. Some scientists think that these monkeys use the colors to send signals to one another through the thick forest.

The gorilla is one of our closest relatives. Movies such as *King Kong* have shown

A family of mountain gorillas

gorillas as fierce and violent
animals. Actually, gorillas are
very peaceful and gentle if

they are not disturbed. They live in small groups and spend their days searching for the leaves and plants they like to eat.

Gorillas are now becoming endangered as their Central African rain-forest habitat is destroyed. Many conservation groups are looking for ways to save gorillas in the wild.

Chimpanzees are among the most intelligent primates. Many of their facial expressions are

Chimpanzees are very intelligent.

like ours. And, like people, chimps can use tools. They have even been seen "fishing" for termites by poking a long twig into a termite nest, pulling the twig out, and licking off the termites that cling to it.

An adult chimpanzee showing a young chimpanzee how to use a "fishing" tool

Animals of the Savanna

If you visited an East African savanna, you would surely see a pride of lions. Most members of the cat family prefer to live alone, but lions live in groups. The males protect the pride and the females do the hunting. But when the females catch prey,

A pride of lions

Although the female lions do the hunting, the male lions get to eat first.

the males get to eat first, even though the females have done most of the work!

The cheetah is the fastest of the big cats. When sprinting after prey, a cheetah can reach a top speed of 70 mi. (113 km) per hour. However, it can run at this speed for only about 30 seconds at a time before it has to slow down and take a rest.

The cheetah is the world's fastest land animal over short distances.

Great Traveling Wildebeests!

One of the most amazing sights in East Africa is the yearly wildebeest migration. During the dry season, tens of thousands of wildebeests walk nearly 1,000 m (1,609 km) in search of food and water.

For a zebra, gazelle, or wildebeest, the savanna can be a dangerous place. Since there is nowhere to hide, these animals depend on their keen eyesight and great hearing to warn them when danger is near. Strange as it seems, the boldly striped zebra hides best by standing in a group of other zebras. In the middle of all those black-and-white stripes, it's hard for a lion or

Zebras hide best from predators by standing in a group of other zebras.

other predator to pick out any particular zebra.

Elephants and rhinoceroses are the largest mammals on the African plains. Both have long been hunted by humans— elephants for their ivory tusks

A herd of African elephants (top) and a rhinoceros mother and calf (bottom)

and rhinos for their horns. As a result, both these animals are endangered and may one day be found only in zoos.

Saving Africa's Animals

Hunting is not the only threat African animals face. Another problem is that the lands where these animals live are being destroyed. Savannas are being turned into farmland or cities. Forests are being cut down because people want to use

Rhinoceroses near Nairobi, Kenya (above), and a logger cutting down a tree in a West African rain forest (right)

the trees to build new houses and want to turn the land into

Cropland at the edge
of an African forest

pastures. Every day, there is
less space for African wildlife.

People can help endangered
African animals by passing laws
to stop people from hunting
them. We can also create parks

and wildlife reserves where the animals will be safe. Visit your local zoo to learn more about these endangered animals and what you can do to help save them.

National parks, like this one in southern Africa, help protect Africa's wildlife.

To Find Out More

Here are some additional resources to help you learn more about African animals:

 **Books**

Arnold, Caroline. **African Animals.** William Morrow & Company, 1997.

Bateman, Robert. **Safari.** Little Brown & Company, 1998.

Dorros, Arthur. **Rain Forest Secrets.** Scholastic, Inc., 1990.

Few, Roger. **Children's Guide to Endangered Animals.** Macmillan, 1993.

Halliburt, Warren J. **African Wildlife**. Crestwood House, 1992.

Saign, Geoffrey C. **The African Cats.** Franklin Watts, 1999.

Organizations and Online Sites

Animal Planet
http://www.Animal. Discovery.com

Information on all kinds of animals, as well as links to nature shows on the Discovery Channel.

National Geographic
http://www.national geographic.com

Lots of interesting information on animals and nature for kids and adults.

Serengeti Stories
http://www.pbs.org/wnet/ nature/serengeti/

Learn about the wildlife of the Serengeti at this PBS site.

Wildlife Conservation Society
http://www.wcs.org

The website of the Wildlife Conservation Society, which operates the Bronx Zoo in New York, offers information on conservation of endangered animals.

Important Words

conservation protection

continent one of the major land masses of Earth

crustacean animal with a hard, outer shell, such as a crab or lobster

endangered in danger of dying out

grazing feeding on plants

habitat place where an animal or plant naturally lives or grows

migration movement of an animal or group of animals from one place to another

predator animal that hunts other animals

prey animal hunted by another for food

pride group of lions

primate group of mammals that includes humans, apes, and monkeys

Index

Meet the Author

Ann O. Squire has a Ph.D. in animal behavior. Before becoming a writer, she studied rats, African electric fish, and other animals. Dr. Squire has written several books on animals and their behavior, including *Anteaters, Sloths, and Armadillos* and *Spiders of North America*. She lives with her children, Emma and Evan, in Bedford, New York.

Photographs ©: Animals Animals: 9 top (Joe McDonald), 9 bottom (Barbara Von Hoffmann); Earth Scenes: 8 (Ashod Francis); ENP Images: 7 bottom right, 19 top, 31, 36, 38, 39, 41 top (Gerry Ellis); Peter Arnold Inc.: 33 (T. Arthus-Bertrand), 4 (Denis-Hout/Bios), 7 top (S.J. Krasemann), 2 (Gerard Lacz), 10 top (Klaus Paysan), 15 (M.&C. Photography), (Malcolm Boulton), 42 (Mark Boulton), cover (Tim Davis), 17 top (E.R. Degginger), 10 bottom, 13 (Nigel J. Dennis), 19 bottom (Nigel J. Dennis/NHPA), 43 (Clem Haagner), 34 (Clem Haagner/ABPL), 12 bottom, 28 (Martin Harvey/NHPA), 41 bottom (Jacques Jangoux), 26 (G.C. Kelley), 22 (Tom & Pat Leeson), 24 (Tom Mchugh), 17 bottom (Mark Smith), 1, 7 bottom left (Art Wolfe).
Map by Joe Le Monnier.